# Animals in SUMMER

A tiny deer mouse nibbles on summer's tasty blackberries.

By Jane R. McCauley

## NATIONAL GEOGRAPHIC SOCIETY

Washington, D.C.

**S**ummer spreads across the land, slowly melting snow off the mountains. Two children see a deer that is growing a new set of antlers. Summer is a busy time for animals.

A box turtle stretches its neck and smells the air on a sunny day. Another snacks on wild strawberries. In summer, turtles find a lot of berries, worms, and insects to eat.

In the spring or early summer, the female turtle laid eggs in a hole she dug. After covering them with dirt, she left them to hatch later in the summer.

**S**cram! A female goose flaps her wings and hisses at a skunk that has come near her nest.

The skunk might be a mother trying to take the eggs to feed her own young. Do you think the goose can scare the skunk away?

**B**aby geese, called goslings, follow their mother into a pond. Like many other baby animals, they grow up in summer. By fall, the goslings will be almost as big as their mother.

One by one, baby box turtles and king snakes wiggle out of their shells. The babies are on their own as soon as they hatch. Their mothers wandered off after laying the eggs.

Only one week old, they can already swim.
The goslings can get their own food, too, but
they still need their mother nearby.

At the edge of a swamp, a mother deer keeps a lookout as her fawn takes a drink of water. The fawn will not leave its mother until next year. For now, it learns how to find food and stay alert for danger by watching what she does.

All day and night in summer, the buzzing and humming of insects fill the air. The polka-dot insects do not sing. They are ladybird beetles, also called ladybugs. They eat other insects such as aphids. Tiny red aphids suck juices from a plant. Some of the aphids have wings.
Can you find the one on this plant that has wings?

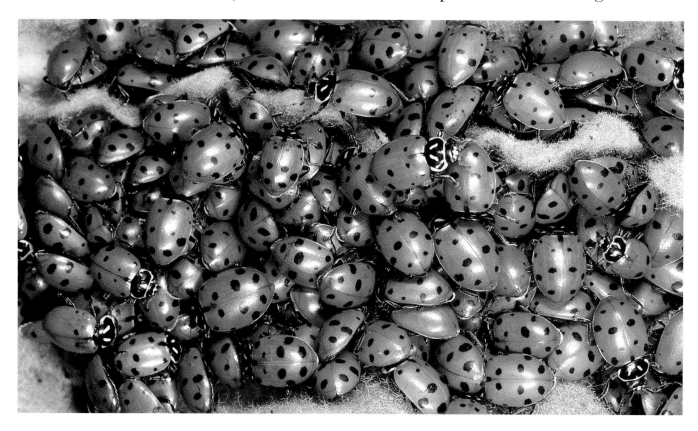

A cicada has just shed its "skin." Soon it will harden and look like the cicadas hanging on the leaves. You can hear the loud song of cicadas in summer.

12

Birds need to catch a lot of insects to feed the young that were hatched in spring. A baby redstart stays snug beside its parent in the nest. The little bird is helpless and cannot open its eyes yet. Its feathers have not all grown in.

A yellow warbler drops an insect into the mouth of one of its young. For days the baby birds will just chirp and eat. But in less than two weeks, they will fly off alone.

Young animals are up in the trees, down in the meadow, just about everywhere late in summer. A gray wolf pup that goes off to play keeps in touch with its mother by howling. This helps her find the pup if an enemy comes near.

As young animals grow older, they begin to explore. A bear cub climbs a pine tree and licks the bark. The cub holds on with its sharp claws. Bear cubs play in the trees. They also go up them to sniff out honey and to escape danger.

Peekaboo! A squirrel hides out in its tree hole. Young raccoons may find shelter in dens on the ground. In the water they catch fish and frogs to eat.

How lazy a bullfrog looks
as it floats on the water.
The frog spends some of its day
on land, waiting to catch insects.
It is still growing. In a few days,
the little tail on top of its back
will disappear.

Turtles living in a pond often
warm their bodies in the sun
during the day. Sometimes they
crawl out on a log. They poke
their heads out and look around.

Wherever there are ponds or streams, you can find animals in summer. A black-and-white warbler hops in the water, then rolls on his side with a splash. The warbler is cleaning his feathers. Maybe he's cooling off. Birds bathe all year long, but they do it more often when the weather is hot and dry.

Animals get thirsty on a hot day. A chipmunk leans over to drink from a quiet stream. You might see a chipmunk at a puddle in the woods after a summer shower.

**W**hoosh! Thousands of bats leave their cave at sunset to find insects to eat. Another kind of bat uses its long tongue to sip liquid from a flower. In almost the same way, a moth drinks from a zinnia. As the bat and the moth fly from flower to flower, they carry yellow dust, or pollen, on their bodies.

Many animals live in a swamp. A green-backed heron holds a sunfish in its bill. The bird returns to the swamp each summer because it can find insects and fish to eat. A green tree frog munches a dragonfly it caught.

With its long bill, a limpkin reaches into the shell of an apple snail. This swamp bird eats almost nothing else.

Autumn is finally on the way! The little pika gathers a pile of leaves and stems to store for winter. Squirrels stuff themselves with food. One bites into a mushroom. Another buries nuts.

Summer is a wonderful season for all creatures. As it comes to an end, they work hard to stay warm and well-fed through the winter.

# MORE ABOUT Animals in Summer

As the long, hot days of summer arrive, meadows and woodlands are alive with animal activity. Swarms of insects whirl in the air, baby birds chirp, and spiders spin webs. Vacations and outdoor activities such as hiking, fishing, and camping offer families the chance to observe a variety of creatures. For most of the animals, summer is the season for raising young.

Why do we have summer? The seasons change as the earth makes its yearly journey around the sun on a tilted axis. From March 20 to September 23, the northern hemisphere is tipped toward the sun, bringing higher temperatures and longer days to this part of the world. Summer weather is not the same everywhere, however; and along with variations of the weather come differences in animal behavior. Snow melts slowly in the mountains (2-3),* and cold weather lingers. Creatures in the mountains may not emerge from their winter retreats as early as they do elsewhere.

The abundance of food in summer and added hours of daylight for foraging provide favorable conditions for growing up. Egg laying for many species usually occurs in spring, and hatching of the young takes place as the warm weather sets in.

In many areas, box turtles (4-5, 8) hatch from eggs that were buried in the ground by the female in late spring and early summer. When they are ready to hatch about three months later, the baby turtles tear at the eggshells, using an egg tooth. These sharp little projections on their noses eventually fall off. Next, the turtles must make their way out of their underground nest, a process that can take several days. Once above the ground, the turtles are able to feed themselves and move about, but they are still vulnerable to predators until their outer shells are more developed.

Sharing the woods with box turtles are king snakes (8), which also must fend for themselves as soon as they hatch. In spring the female snake hides her eggs under leaves or logs or in the soil. This protects the embryos and provides them with warmth and moisture. By late summer the snakes are ready to come out of their leathery shells. They, too, tear them open with an egg tooth. The snakes stay in the shells for a few more days, drawing nourishment from the remains of the yolk.

Other young animals rely on their parents for protection and guidance for weeks or longer. Fawns (cover, 10-11), for example, tag along with their mothers for up to two years and learn by copying them.

Birds that are altricial, such as the warbler (14), are blind, featherless, and require constant care at first. With their parents tending them, they develop quickly. They leave the nest within two weeks. Even baby animals that are able to do many things at first need their parents for guidance. Precocial birds, such as geese (8-9), can see, walk, and feed themselves just after hatching. Instinctively, however, they follow their parents, depending on them to lead them to food.

Just as children do, young animals like to explore in the summertime. A wolf pup may wander into a meadow full of flowers (16-17). Bear cubs (18) climb trees with their sharp claws, sometimes in search of bees' honey.

*Yellow pollen sticks to a bumblebee's leg as the bee sips nectar from an aster. By carrying pollen from flower to flower, the bee helps plants reproduce.*

Animals have ways of coping with summer heat. Some wallow in mud. Others seek shade. Certain animals respond to excessive heat by aestivating, entering a dormant state. One kind of frog burrows underground and sheds a layer of skin, which covers the frog and helps seal in moisture. Other animals, such as warblers (22-23), deal with heat by bathing often. Besides helping them cool off, bathing conditions their feathers by stimulating oil secretion. And it gets rid of parasites.

While some animals avoid heat, others seek it out. Painted turtles (21)—a common aquatic species—

*Numbers in parentheses refer to pages in *Animals in Summer*.

depend on the sun for body heat. Like all reptiles, they are cold-blooded and unable to control their internal temperature. The turtles warm themselves by taking brief sunbaths. As summer wanes and the temperature goes down, the turtles grow sluggish, eventually becoming inactive.

Early in summer tadpoles develop near the water's edge. Most turn rapidly into frogs (27) as they grow lungs and legs. A large bullfrog (20), however, can take more than a year to mature. The deep calls of the bullfrog can often be heard on a summer evening.

The buzzing of insects can be heard day or night. Among the loudest is the cicada (12). The immature cicada grows for years in the ground, protected by a tough exoskeleton. It emerges from the ground, climbs a tree, and sheds its exoskeleton on the trunk. After a brief mating season, the cicada dies in a few weeks.

The female garden spider mates in late summer. She encloses her eggs in a case she spins of silk from her body, and dies soon afterward. The young hatch, then remain quietly in their protective sac in the web until the following spring. In contrast, green lynx spiderlings leave their egg sac before winter and hibernate under bark or a leaf. They spin thin strands of silk, which are easily caught by breezes. The spiderlings may ride the silken strands for some miles.

Spiders benefit from the many insects available in summer, as do tree frogs (27), turtles, birds, and bats (24-25). At twilight bats fly out from their homes in caves and other places to search for insects. Other kinds of bats sip nectar from flowers, spreading pollen at the same time.

The prevalence of food in this season lures birds like the green-

On a June day, a nanny and her kid look down from a high ridge. The adult mountain goat has shed most of her shaggy winter coat.

backed heron (26) to the same marsh each year. The heron dips into the water to jab small fish with its sharp, pointed beak.

Without summer's bounty, many animals could not survive a harsh winter. Squirrels (19, 28) storing nuts in the ground and in tree holes is a familiar sight as the days begin to shorten. Even earlier, pikas (28-29) scurry across mountainsides, cutting and gathering stems and roots of plants, which they lay in the sun to dry. Pikas build haystacks, often several feet tall, beside their homes in the rocks. During snowstorms a pika just steps out of its home to reach the food.

Whether you go to the mountains or to the seashore, or stay close to home, you'll be sure to discover busy animals in summer. The following activities can guide you and your children in observing the animals in your area. If you live where there are no marked seasonal differences, you may want to compare the cycle of creatures around you to those in other regions of the country. At what time of year, for example, do you see baby birds hatching?

Select a tree or a space near your home and study the habits of the creatures living there. What do they eat? When do they rest? Do they have young? If so, try to follow their development. *But do not disturb the animals or their homes.*

See how many kinds of insects you can spot, but be careful not to touch them. Some may sting or bite. Record in a notebook what they look like or draw pictures of them. What sounds do they make? Then borrow an insect book from your library to identify them. Look up the differences between insects and spiders.

Choose an animal you like such as a bird or raccoon. Write a story or draw pictures of how it spends its summer. At your library gather books to help you learn more about your creature. What does it do at other times of the year? Does it migrate or hibernate?

If you or a friend have a dog or a cat, you can observe ways animals survive heat in summer. Does the pet pant a lot, move around less, or sit in the shade? Does it drink a lot of water? What do *you* do to stay cool in summer?

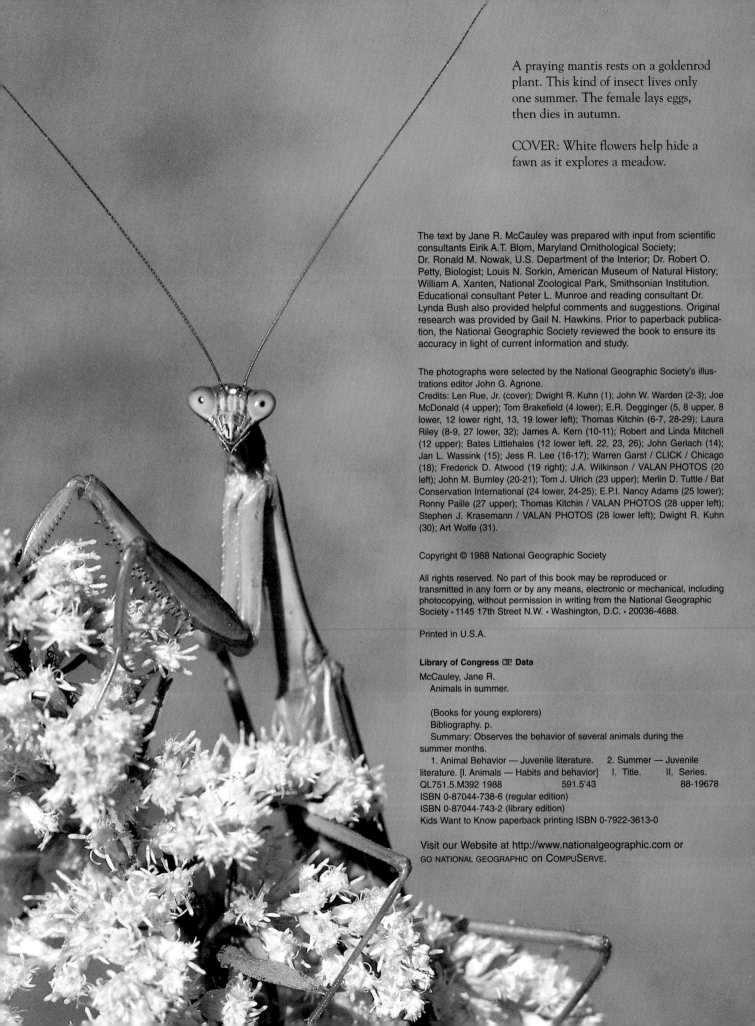

A praying mantis rests on a goldenrod plant. This kind of insect lives only one summer. The female lays eggs, then dies in autumn.

COVER: White flowers help hide a fawn as it explores a meadow.

The text by Jane R. McCauley was prepared with input from scientific consultants Eirik A.T. Blom, Maryland Ornithological Society; Dr. Ronald M. Nowak, U.S. Department of the Interior; Dr. Robert O. Petty, Biologist; Louis N. Sorkin, American Museum of Natural History; William A. Xanten, National Zoological Park, Smithsonian Institution. Educational consultant Peter L. Munroe and reading consultant Dr. Lynda Bush also provided helpful comments and suggestions. Original research was provided by Gail N. Hawkins. Prior to paperback publication, the National Geographic Society reviewed the book to ensure its accuracy in light of current information and study.

The photographs were selected by the National Geographic Society's illustrations editor John G. Agnone.
Credits: Len Rue, Jr. (cover); Dwight R. Kuhn (1); John W. Warden (2-3); Joe McDonald (4 upper); Tom Brakefield (4 lower); E.R. Degginger (5, 8 upper, 8 lower, 12 lower right, 13, 19 lower left); Thomas Kitchin (6-7, 28-29); Laura Riley (8-9, 27 lower, 32); James A. Kern (10-11); Robert and Linda Mitchell (12 upper); Bates Littlehales (12 lower left, 22, 23, 26); John Gerlach (14); Jan L. Wassink (15); Jess R. Lee (16-17); Warren Garst / CLICK / Chicago (18); Frederick D. Atwood (19 right); J.A. Wilkinson / VALAN PHOTOS (20 left); John M. Burnley (20-21); Tom J. Ulrich (23 upper); Merlin D. Tuttle / Bat Conservation International (24 lower, 24-25); E.P.I. Nancy Adams (25 lower); Ronny Paille (27 upper); Thomas Kitchin / VALAN PHOTOS (28 upper left); Stephen J. Krasemann / VALAN PHOTOS (28 lower left); Dwight R. Kuhn (30); Art Wolfe (31).

Printed in U.S.A.

**Library of Congress ⊂ℙ Data**
McCauley, Jane R.
   Animals in summer.

   (Books for young explorers)
   Bibliography. p.
   Summary: Observes the behavior of several animals during the summer months.
   1. Animal Behavior — Juvenile literature.   2. Summer — Juvenile literature. [I. Animals — Habits and behavior]   I. Title.   II. Series.
QL751.5.M392 1988          591.5′43          88-19678
ISBN 0-87044-738-6 (regular edition)
ISBN 0-87044-743-2 (library edition)
Kids Want to Know paperback printing ISBN 0-7922-3613-0

Visit our Website at http://www.nationalgeographic.com or GO NATIONAL GEOGRAPHIC on COMPUSERVE.